GONE WAY DOWN

TEENAGE DRUG-USE IS A DISEASE

By
MILLER NEWTON, Ph.D.

Illustrations by Shawn Arnow

AMERICAN STUDIES PRESS
Tampa, Florida

International Standard Book No. 0-934996-16-4
Library of Congress Catalog Card No. 81-52441

Published by

AMERICAN STUDIES PRESS
13511 Palmwood Lane
Tampa, Florida 33624

Printed in the United States of America

DEDICATION

This book is dedicated to the kids and families of STRAIGHT, INC., who had the care and courage to do something about their problem, and whose fearless and searching honesty made this book possible.

CONTENTS

ACKNOWLEDGEMENTS ════════════════════════

I am grateful to the many, many people whose lives and words have influenced my personal journey to STRAIGHT, INC. In particular, I am grateful for the help of the following peer staff members at **Straight, Inc.**, who gave time and care to reading the manuscript, raising tough questions and staying with me until we got answers: Chris, Dave, Mark, Shawn, Jim, William, Brett, Kathleen, and Kerry. Their honest comments made this book real. I am also grateful to all the members of the Group at **Straight** whose honesty about themselves provided the basic data for this description of drug-use as a disease.

This book comes out of the heart of **Straight, Inc.** I appreciate Jim Hartz, the Executive Director, and the Board of **Straight, Inc.**, whose dedication continues to make the Program possible. They have given me the opportunity for significant and worthwhile work. In addition, Laura Morgan and Bill Giesz, professional staff members, have read and reread the manuscript with care, critique, and helpful comments. The members of my doctoral committee also contributed at a later stage in the development of the manuscript. My thanks go to Roger Ortmayer, Jean Battle, Marilyn Persons, and Margaret Holland. Their conceptual critique helped me move the manuscript to a higher level.

Patricia Plastic, Kathy Hermann, and Carolyn Duncan helped with the typing at various stages. My special gratitude goes to Linda Evans who typed the manuscript again and again. Her care for form, grammar and content, contributed immensely to the quality of the work. She lived with this project for many months. Sharon Sutter, Cindy Watson, Maryellen Alexanderwicz, and Suzanne Byrd provided editorial critique and assistance at important points in the manuscript's development. My thanks to American Studies Press and Don Harkness for seeing value in this book and publishing it.

Most importantly, this book is because of Mark, who became a victim of drug-use and whose problem brought us to **Straight**. His recovery gave me the motivation to share with others what I had learned. Ruth Ann, my wife, his mother, and the finest chemical dependency counselor I know, brought the family to the place where we could understand and act on Mark's problem. Her career meant being at the right place at the right time. In addition, her awareness, sensitivity, and intuition all contributed to my growing knowledge which led to *Gone Way Down*. I am also grateful to Miller IV and Johanna for their commitment to their brother, to our family getting straight, and to **Straight, Inc.** This is a family story.

INTRODUCTION

Teenage drug-use is America's fastest growing health problem. The National Institute of Drug Abuse (NIDA) in its studies estimates one out of every five high school young people "does drugs" on a regular, weekday basis. However, the kids in **Straight, Inc.** say the figure is much higher, up to one out of every two. The young people gave us figures for their high schools that range from 40% to 56% of the student population on consistent use during the school week. When you add the number of young people who "do drugs" in a social setting on weekends (the kids call them "weekend warriors"), the percentages increase considerably. Not only the data, but also my experience with kids on drugs leads to an alarming picture of the current generation of young people.

The purpose of this book is to provide information for parents, helping professionals, and others, about adolescent drug-use in America today. My hope is that the disease etiology presented here will help adults make sense out of what they are experiencing with young people in their families and in their organizations.

Chapter 1
BACKGROUND

This book really began in January, 1979, when my wife and I discovered that our youngest son, aged 15, had a drug problem. At the time, both of us were working in the alcohol rehabilitation field. I served as Executive Director of Florida Alcohol Coalition, and my wife was a Team Leader (Supervising Counselor) with Alcohol Community Treatment Services in Tampa, Florida. Our two older children were achieving "straight" kids who had reached their early twenties without difficulty. We attempted to deal with our son's drug-use ourselves for six months. Another crisis helped us realize our inability to deal with our son's drug-use. We found **Straight, Inc.** and began our recovery as a family.

Thinking back to that six-month period from the first crisis to admission into **Straight, Inc.,** I recall how little I knew about teenage drug-use. Both my wife and I knew a good deal about adult alcoholism and its treatment, but my personal view about drug-use involved only images of slum heroin addicts from the 50's and hippies, or "flower children," from the 60's. The "flower-child" image, which involved drug-use as a quest for higher religious consciousness and revolt against middle-class America's values, was particularly misleading. Some parents of current adolescents have the same misconceptions. Others have accepted the view that drug-use is a harmless recreational pastime. Still others have overwhelming fear due to almost total ignorance about drug-use.

My involvement at **Straight, Inc.,** first as a parent, later as Assistant Director and then as Director, was a process of discovery about current adolescent drug-use. Teenage drug-use today is a distinct and different phenomenon from either the

50's or the 60's. My personal quest for knowledge also involved helping other parents and helping professionals understand the teenage drug scene.

The material in this book was originally developed as a presentation for the new parent orientation process at **Straight, Inc.,** a private, not-for-profit drug rehabilitation program in St. Petersburg, Florida. It has been in existence for almost five years. The Program incorporates Alcoholic Anonymous' tools and process for personal change, a peer-counseling concept, family systems theory, and rational behavioral therapy.

The Program has emphasized intensive large group peer pressure as a modality for treatment and total family involvement. Early in 1980, a new process was designed for integrating new parents into the treatment program. This involves six New Parent Raps over the first three weeks of the child's program. The intent of the Raps is to allow parents to express their feelings about the "insane" experience they had been through with their children and then to find a coherent rational framework in which to understand their child's and their own behavior. The families then go on to understanding how the illness infects the total family system and how the total family needs treatment. The material in this book was developed to provide that coherent rational framework for staff and parents' understanding of the young person's problem.

Since the founding of **Straight, Inc.** five years ago, about 2,000 young people have entered the Program. The majority have been from a six-county area making up the Tampa Bay metropolitan area. Others have come from the Miami/Fort Lauderdale metropolitan area, the Florida Keys, Fort Myers, Naples, Orlando, Jacksonville, Daytona Beach, Pensacola, and ten other Florida counties. We have also had large concentrations of clients from the Atlanta and Cincinnati metropolitan areas. In addition, families have come from Massachusetts, New York, New Jersey, Maryland, Virginia, North Carolina,

Alabama, Michigan, California, Texas, and Alaska. The data upon which this description of drug-use is based, therefore, comes from a sufficiently widespread area of the United States to make it generalizable. The data has come from the young people once they are far enough along in the Program that staff members feel their honesty is credible.

The research techniques I used were those developed by ethnographic researchers in anthropology. I have used a variety of techniques, including structured interviews with the teenagers, participant observation of the therapy group, structured interviews with parents and other adults significant in the lives of the children, and some structured situation re-enactments. The data has been developed over a twelve-month period of time and represents information from almost eight hundred young people. I have tested my observations and conclusions with members of the peer counseling staff, as well as with the adult professional staff. Their combined experience with teenagers in the Program goes back to the very beginning of the Program.

The presentation that follows is in part an adaptation of the "Disease of Feelings" etiology, originally developed by Johnson Institute in Minneapolis to describe adult alcoholism. I am indebted to Vern Johnson and to the staff of the Johnson Institute for their work. I have modified and adapted the etiology to fit the pattern for teenagers' drug-use.

Chapter 2
DRUG-USE vs. DRUG ABUSE ════════════════

Whenever I hear someone talk about drug abuse, I get funny pictures in my mind. I think of a kid with a stick beating "a plastic baggie of grass" lying on the ground. I picture a kid jumping up and down on a plastic bottle of pills, grinding them into the sidewalk with his heel. These pictures may be a personal quirk, but they point to a very important distinction. Teenagers "use drugs." In using drugs, teenagers abuse themselves.

Personal abuse involves the guilt and shame which lead to a deteriorating sense of personal self-worth. This self-abuse involves behavior that gets kids into trouble. It also involves family relationships filled with anger, static, and hurt. It involves the loss of dreams about education, work, and future marital relationships. It involves trouble with adult authorities — in particular, the law.

"Drug abuse" implies that it is OK to use mood-altering drugs up to a certain point. It implies that use beyond that "limit" is trouble. However, if you can keep your use within those "limits," then you're OK. This is a message that a large part of the adult world gives kids. Teachers, entertainment personalities, even people in some drug abuse rehabilitation facilities tell kids that if they will keep their drinking and "smoking" outside of school and work hours, that it's OK, it's acceptable to use drugs. My experience is that kids who use drugs find themselves increasingly unable to control their use of the drugs and their behavior as a result of that use. Therefore, I believe that any use of mood-altering chemicals by adolescents is by definition self-abuse. Drug-use itself is the problem, is the disease.

There are two cultural values in America that encourage

use of mood-altering chemicals. Teenagers in the process of acculturation, that is, learning our society's values, tune in to these two values. The first is approved use of alcohol. I, as an individual, and **Straight, Inc.,** as a Program, define alcohol as a mood-altering drug. Our society has enshrined alcohol in the rituals of our life as a people. Alcohol is a "necessary" lubricant for social gatherings, from sophisticated upper-middle-class cocktail parties to working-class picnics. Business is conducted over two-martini lunches. Rituals of birth, graduation, marriage, and death, all take place with the necessary and appropriate alcoholic beverages. Our society tells kids that drinking is not only acceptable, but that it is necessary and good. We even convey the notion that it is OK to feel "in the pink" and to get "smashing" drunk.

The second cultural value that encourages use of drugs comes from the medical world. All of us experience physical pain in the course of our lifetime. Pain is an alarm or warning system, telling us that something is wrong. The symptomatic warning should lead to medical assistance in solving the basic problem. However, our society believes that one should not suffer physical pain. The medical doctor in the usual course of treatment prescribes not only medication for the cause of the pain, but often a pain killer as well. The notion that "a good doctor stops you from hurting" is deeply embedded in the core of our values about life and illness. It extends beyond physical pain to emotional pain as well. The general practitioner, the family doctor, often dispenses tranquilizers for people who are depressed, unhappy, or upset. Some doctors also liberally prescribe tranquilizers for adults going through a life crisis. The family practitioner may be encouraging promiscuous use of mood-altering drugs by prescribing tranquilizers and pain killers. Prescription of these drugs suggest to our young people that pain is bad and that you should always "feel good."

Both of these cultural values encourage our youth to use alcohol and other drugs promiscuously for pleasure and to avoid pain. "Life is about 'feeling good,' and chemicals are a shortcut to good feelings."

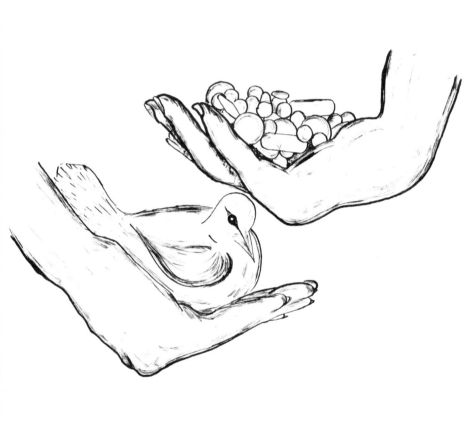

Chapter 3
DRUG-USE IS A DISEASE OF CHOICE

When parents first arrive at **Straight, Inc.**, they bring a lot of guilt about their personal failure with their children. Somehow they expect to find some grand defect in themselves to explain why their child drinks, smokes pot, and "does" other drugs. This attitude is great for the kid, who can use his/her parent's guilt as an excuse to get "high."

On the first night of New Parent Raps, we usually begin quite seriously by asking the parents, "Did any of you buy marijuana for your child? Did you roll the joint and light it? Did you hold the child down, stuff it in his mouth, and pump his chest so that he would inhale? Did you buy the six-pack of beer, hold his mouth open, and pour it down his throat?" Of course not. It's absurd to think that any of the parents who bring kids to our Program did this. They did not cause their child to use drugs.

The next question is always, "Who or what caused my child to use drugs?" We all have a need for some grand social failure and/or defect to explain teenage drug-use. I have searched the social histories of our families at **Straight, Inc.** in vain for a common factor or factors which cause the children's drug-use.

Each young person makes his or her own choice to drink and to smoke pot. Adolescence is a period during which the child experiences a strong need to belong to his/her peer group. Usually the choice is in response to pressure from peers. Beginning use of mood-altering chemicals is clearly a personal choice. As a matter of fact, most children (nine out of ten) do not like the taste of beer or marijuana the first four to six times that they use the chemicals. They keep forcing themselves to drink and to smoke against the unpleasant taste. Four out of five kids tell us they used pot at least four times before their first "high." In time, they learn to get the high, euphoric feeling that comes from the mood-altering quality of the chemicals. You need to understand that drug-use is a disease initiated by personal choice in response to peer pressure. The kid has to do something himself to get sick. Once he/she has made the initial choice, it becomes a disease because he/she progressively loses control of his feelings, his behavior, his physical health, and even his own use of the chemicals.

Not only is it important for an understanding of the disease to recognize the personal choice element, but it is also critically important to the treatment process. Each child and family needs to recognize the child's personal responsibilty for doing drugs, because personal choice, a decision to "get straight," is a vital part of recovery.

Chapter 4
CHARACTERISTICS OF THE DISEASE ════════

After the child has made the choice to "do" drugs, the progressive loss of control of feelings, behavior, and the drug-use itself has a characteristic pattern. Drug-use is a disease because it is primary, chronic, progressive, and terminal.

Drug-Use Is A Primary Disease.

About three-quarters of the children who come to our Program have been seen for long periods of time by psychiatrists, psychologists, school counselors, and pediatricians. They have been treated for almost every known emotional problem and for many physical symptoms as well. Most of the other professionals have tended to treat drug-use itself as a symptom of some other real and basic problem. This misunderstanding is partially due to confusion in recent decades. about norms for healthy adolescent behavior. No matter how intensive the treatment has been, it changes neither what was considered to be the real problem, nor the drug-use. The message is quite simple: the use of drugs itself is a primary illness. Motivation problems, mood and behavior problems, family problems, and chronic lung cough are symptoms of the presence of alien chemicals in the child's body chemistry when drug-use is involved. Disturbed family relationships, loss of motivation, and physical illnesses cannot be treated effectively until the child's body chemistry is drug-free and the child develops the personal skills necessary to remain drug-free. When drug-use is the disease that must be treated, all the other problems are symptoms.

Drug-Use Is A Chronic Disease.

One of the most difficult problems we face at **Straight, Inc.** is the refusal of parents to accept the fact that drug-use is a long-term, noncurable disease. They want so much for Johnny to be able to have a "normal" life. Johnny should be able to drink beer with the boys in his fraternity at college. When he grows up, he should be able to go to cocktail parties, drink wine with his meals, and do business over martinis. Diabetes, though its cause is different, is another example of a chronic disease. Like the diabetic, the "druggie" can have a healthy and happy life as long as he does the necessary things in his lifestyle to remain drug-free. He may never drink, smoke marijuana, nor use even prescribed mood-altering drugs. Like an alcoholic, he cannot use any mood-altering chemical without risking his health and life. Any use of drugs will trigger again for him the progressive and deteriorating disease process.

Drug-Use Is A Progressive Disease.

Some people naively believe that kids can smoke a little pot, drink socially, or use pills occasionally. Once most kids begin the use of mood-altering chemicals, a process begins involving feelings, behavior, self-worth, and use of the drugs themselves that is progressive. The progression is from mild use of drugs with few emotional consequences, to increasingly deteriorating feelings, behavior, and ego strength.

The kids recognize the progression in their own slang language. "Lines" are crossed in use of drugs themselves. The children describe crossing those lines as "moving up." One line is between pot/alcohol and pills ("ups" and "downs"). The next line is from pot, alcohol, and pills, "up" to "hard drugs" (acid, coke, P.C.P., M.D.A., etc.). The final line is crossed when you begin "shooting up"; that is, injecting drugs. The self-deception involved in "moving up" is "everyone else is doing it and it's not hurting them," and "I'll try the harder drug just once." Of course, the child always does it again.

The children also use descriptive titles for different states in drug-use. "Bop" is a pot- and alcohol-user; "Stonie" ("Stoner") is a regular pot- and pill-user; and "Freak" or "Burnout" is a compulsive and harder drug-user. "Pot-heads" to "Druggies" to "Junkies" is a similar sequence of titles. The slang titles also document the progressive nature of the disease.

He's "gone way down" is what the kids say about a friend who has "moved up" faster than themselves. His appearance and life have deteriorated, while his drug-use has increased. The kids also use "gone way down" as a self-description when looking back at their drug-using past from the vantage point of recovery. They recognize the progressive deterioration even in street slang.

While the progression occurs over different periods of time for different people, it is, nevertheless, relentless. Adolescents cannot maintain mild or occasional drug-use patterns. They get worse. The progression may involve harder drugs or may simply involve heavier and more regular use of pot and alcohol. However, the effect is the same. You've "gone way down."

Drug-Use Is A Terminal Disease.

The final result of the progressive deterioration in a drug-using person's life is death. There has been an alarming increase in the number of adolescent deaths over the last five years. The leading causes of adolescent death are accident, malignancy (cancer), suicide, and homicide. Three of these causes are obviously drug-use related: accident, suicide, and homicide. The death certificates — which read "accidental death," "cardiac arrest," "aneurysm," "suicide," and "homicide" — often cover up the presence of drugs. Coroners and other doctors mercifully hide the presence of mood-altering drugs as a precipitous cause in an adolescent death situation in order not to further hurt the parents at the time. However, this "act of mercy" ends up masking the alarming dangers associated with drug-use.

My belief is that in the decade or two ahead, those young drug-users who escape overdose, accidental death, or some form of cardiac failure, will have their lives significantly shortened due to other kinds of physiological deterioration. Drug-use is a killer!

Chapter 5
ADDICTION AND HABITUATION

There is a great deal of confusion about the nature of drug-use. Traditionally, we have called someone with a drug-use problem an "addict." That term comes from an earlier era when people with drug-use problems were predominantly heroin users. Times have changed, and drugs have moved from the ghettoes to the suburbs and small towns of America. Drug-use has entered the high school, the junior high school, and even the elementary school. Drugs of preference have changed considerably. Whole new classes of drugs, like P.C.P., an animal tranquilizer often called "Angel Dust," and the hallucinogens have entered the scene. The home medicine cabinet is a warehouse of pain killers, tranquilizers, and other prescription drugs.

Addiction refers to a particular process of drug-use. Drugs are described as addictive if one becomes physically dependent upon the drug. An addicting drug is a chemical compound that with prolonged use becomes part of the normal chemistry of a person's body. When the drug is subsequently withdrawn, the person experiences physiological trauma or shock. For example, alcohol can become part of the balance of chemicals in the body of an individual. When the alcohol is withdrawn, the person experiences physical shock. The person experiences the delirium tremens, sweats, nausea, and other symptoms. Other addicting drugs include the opiates, such as heroin, opium, and morphine. The barbiturate group drugs are also physiologically addictive. Although the young people use the opiates and barbituates on occasion, these addictive drugs are not their preference.

A second process of drug-use is habituation. Habituation is a process in which the individual becomes psychologically dependent upon the drug for ordinary day-to-day living. The habituation process involves learning that the drug will produce certain emotional effects, that is, mood swings. The youngster learns to use the drug to produce "good feelings," often in a recreational setting. In time, the youngster begins to use the drug to deal with moments of feeling bad in order to feel good again. The result is that this person depends on the drugs to function on a day-to-day basis. The drugs become a substitute for the normal emotional coping processes that a healthy person uses to deal with life. Drugs, in addition, become a cause of feeling "down" or "bad," physically and emotionally. A vicious emotional circle is set up that the young person cannot break alone.

Our teenage "druggies" are habituated to drugs rather than addicted. While beer and other alcoholic beverages are preferred drugs, kids have simply not used alcohol long enough to become addicted. The other drug of preference — marijuana — is not addictive. However, marijuana is just as dangerous, because of the effects of habituation with its use. Its psychoactive ingredient, Delta 9-T.H.C., cumulates in the nervous, the respiratory, and the reproductive systems with various resulting damage. Nor are "ups" (amphetamines), "downs" (tranquilizers and sedatives), hallucinogenics (such as LSD) or cocaine, addictive. Most young people use addictive drugs on such rare occasions and usually in moderate amounts, that they do not become addicted.

The difference between addiction and habituation is real medically. Addiction, that is physical dependency on a drug, can be dealt with in a few days by medically supervised detoxification. However, the psychological dependency remains. The destructive effect of this dependency on emotional state, self-worth, and behavior in family and society, is equally serious. There is not a "dime's worth of difference" in the progressive deterioration of life for an addict and a habitué.

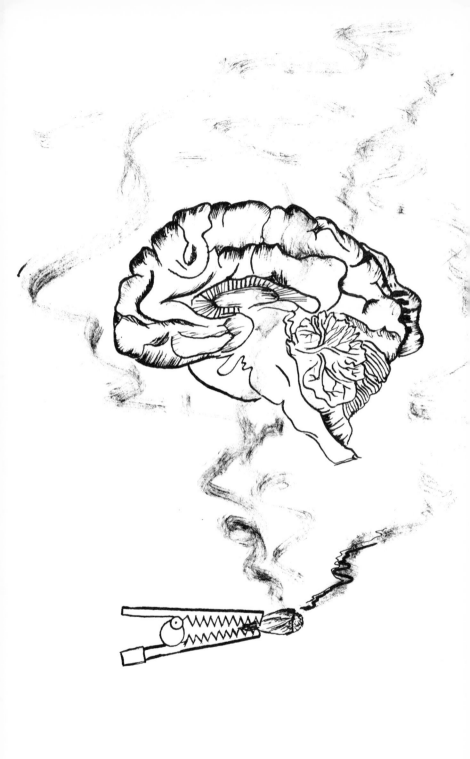

Chapter 6
DRUG-USE IS A DISEASE OF THE FEELINGS

The drugs of preference of today's teenagers all affect the central nervous system; that is, the brain and the spinal cord. Psychoactive drugs primarily affect the "old brain" (limbic system), the center of feeling, rather than the "new brain" (neocortex), the center of conceptualization. As such, they have an effect on the moods that a person experiences while the drugs are active. Some drugs continue to affect feeling long after the "high" is over. The drugs not only affect the mood at the moment, but actually set up a progressive process of changing emotions and feelings in the person's life. Drug-use is clearly a disease of the feelings. The feeling state becomes so distorted that young people who use drugs over a period of time have moments when they feel crazy. Again and again, I hear kids say, "I thought I was going crazy." The thinking process is so distorted that they almost never connect this "crazy" feeling with their drug-use.

On the following page is a simple chart which expresses the nature of human feelings.* The center category is entitled "Normal." This indicates the relatively mild, middle zone of feelings a person experiences in the course of daily living. The middle zone ranges toward pleasure on the top and pain on the bottom. Within this middle zone, the feelings one experiences are mild and tolerable changes in the mood state. The "OK" point in the middle is essentially a neutral feeling where one feels neither good nor bad. The "Euphoria" zone on the top represents extreme pleasurable feelings. It represents a high that is possible through sexual love, through moments of great achievement, through moments of spiritual

*The concept of "The Feeling Chart" is an adaptation from the Johnson Institute.

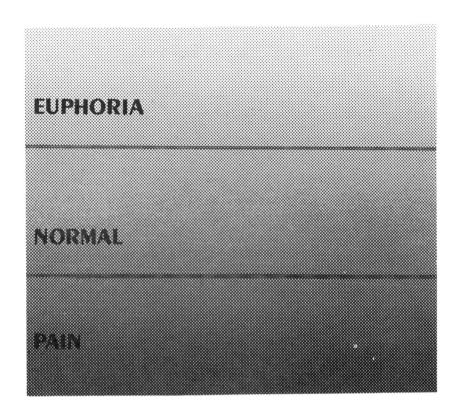

EUPHORIA

NORMAL

PAIN

ecstasy and, also, artificially, through mood-altering drugs. The zone on the bottom, entitled "Pain," represents emotional or feeling pain. This area includes rage, anger, hurt, depression, etc. In the normal course of living, most of the time a person's feeling state remains in the "Normal" zone. In rare moments of achievement or spiritual ecstasy, one ascends into the "Euphoria" zone, and in moments of loss, descends into "Pain." Most of us have developed coping mechanisms to deal with those descents into pain and, also, ways to deal with the moments of rare euphoria. Adolescence is the time when we develop those coping mechanisms which help deal with the mood swings that occur in human life. Drug-use is an artificial shortcut to moods of choice. As such, it interferes with normal development into adulthood.

In the chapters that follow, we will see the progressive

deterioration of the feeling process on the part of a drug-using individual. The experience of emotional change becomes extended and distorted to the point of disrupting his/her life. It involves progressive disruption in every dimension of the child's life: spiritual life, social relationships, productivity and achievement, family life, and physical health. The fact that drug-use affects the normal process of experiencing one's own feelings in such a way as to make one sick, or to make one's behavior "insane," points to the fact that drug-use is indeed a disease.

The four chapters that follow describe in four stages the progressive deterioration caused by drug-use. The stages are characterized by their meaning in terms of the feeling state.

Chapter 7
STAGE ONE –
LEARNING THE MOOD SWING

At the very beginning of drug-use, the youngster is learning that a particular chemical will produce a particular effect. In Stage One, the youngster is being introduced to alcohol and pot, learning how to use it, and learning that it produces a pleasant mood swing. Also, at this stage, the child learns to calibrate his use of chemicals; that is, he learns to produce certain effects by certain amounts of alcohol and/or marijuana. He experiences the excitement of a new, illicit experience.

DRUGS.

In talking to hundreds of adolescents about their initial drug-use, I learned some very interesting facts. Almost every kid was first introduced to drugs in a "party" situation. The young person is "hanging around" with other teenagers, "having fun" when alcohol and/or marijuana is introduced. The kid is pressed to try it in order to be "grown up" and to have a "good time." Nine out of ten kids I have interviewed refused four to six times before their first taste of "booze," or their first "toke" on a joint. Once a child succumbs to the peer pressure of belonging to the group by doing the drug, a second interesting fact occurs: Four out of five teenagers I talked with did not get "high" until the fourth, fifth, sixth, or seventh time that they tried alcohol and/or pot. These two facts suggest that the beginning of drug-use is a learning process on the part of the child. Under the pressure to belong to and be identified with his/her peer group, he/she begins learning to "do" drugs.

The first stage is characterized by the use primarily of pot and alcohol. Most children start with beer and with alcohol from their parents' liquor cabinet. Alcohol use by teenagers forms a fundamentally different pattern from that of adults. Adults drink in moderate doses (sip and swallows) over long periods of time (meals, parties, etc.). The kids "guzzle" one beer or drink after another as quickly as possible to produce a quick "buzz." They drink solely to get drunk.

Some kids "huff" (inhale) glue, Lockerroom/Rush (butyl nitrite) and/or solvents during the first stage. About forty percent of the kids have experimented with inhalants. Of that group, two-thirds "did" inhalants before smoking pot.

The use of these drugs is primarily in a "party" situation with their peers. At this stage, teenagers do not buy their own drugs, but are using drugs that other people have bought. The use is on the weekends and fairly infrequent. The kids get "high" when somebody they are with happens to have some drugs. It is very easy to get "high" at this stage, because infrequent use and small quantity of use makes their tolerance very low. A small amount of the drug produces a rather strong effect emotionally.

BEHAVIOR.

There is no detectable behavior change on the part of the teenager at home, at school, or in any area of his/her life. Because use is spontaneous in a "party" situation, there is no planned deception. The lying occurs only after the fact. This involves simply not saying anything about their experience with drugs. School work, extra-curricular activities, and family life, at this stage, go on normally. The young person may have the slight thrill of doing something "adult" that his/her parents don't know about, but this has little effect on his/her basic emotional state. The difficult problem for parents is the lack of observable behavioral change at this stage.

A certain group of adolescents evidence clear "druggie" behavior and attitudes some time before they actually begin drug-use. Sudden overt changes in dress, friends, and language combined with lying, stealing, rebelliousness, and loss of motivation are clearly signs of identification with the "druggie" peer group. This "need to belong" and the resulting new behavior, is another indication of the initial "learning process" nature of teenage drug-use.

FEELINGS.

Using the feeling chart below, a child, during the Stage One of drug-use, experiences moderate euphoria when he experiences the effect of the drug. The feeling chart shows a movement from "OK" within the Normal zone toward Euphoria, and a return back slightly below the neutral center of the Normal zone. In other words, the youngster has learned that he/she can drink some beer or smoke a joint or

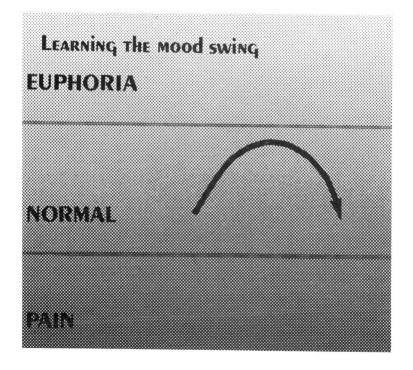

two and feel relaxed, good, and mildly euphoric, with almost no negative consequences. The youngster does not experience real pain afterward, either physically or emotionally. This ability to "feel good" with his/her friends when he/she chooses, with no significant after effects, reinforces the habit of getting "high" on the weekends. It begins the progressive pattern of the disease.

If the adult world, family, school personnel, or others, could detect the youngster's drug-use at this stage, they could intervene, using reason, and possibly stop the youngster's use. Drug-use at this stage is certainly within the realm of possible self-control, but without visible behaviorable consequences, the adult world has no clue that the young person has begun the disease of drug-use.

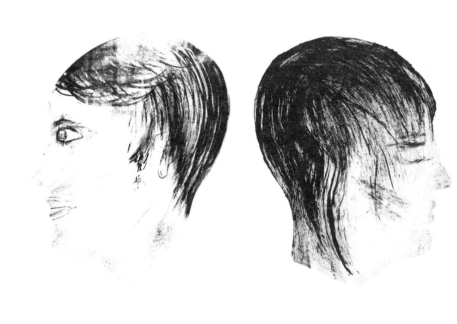

Chapter 8
STAGE TWO –
SEEKING THE MOOD SWING

Having learned that pot and alcohol produce good feelings and that two beers or two joints produce even better
feelings, the teenager moves from spontaneous use to planned
use. Instead of waiting for a "party" situation where friends
have a "bag" of marijuana or a six-pack of beer, the
youngster now starts to take the initiative in securing the
drugs and, also, the privacy necessary to get high.

Stage Two involves the active choice of seeking the mood
swing by "doing" drugs. In a very short time, the youngster
loses control of the choice and *must* have the chemicals to
have good feelings. The movement from active choice to no
choice, characterizes Stage Two.

DRUGS.

Alcohol and pot continue to be the most frequently used
drugs during this stage. In addition, the kids often use hash,
hash oil, Thai stick, and pills. The pills used are "ups"
(amphetamines) and "downs" (tranquilizers and sedatives).
Some kids also begin using hallucinogenic mushrooms (street-
named "Shrooms") very late in this stage. Among the kids
who use "Shrooms," one out of four begin late in this stage.
The other three out of four wait until Stage Three. This
second group expresses fear about "bad trips" with
"Shrooms." The slightly harder drugs that are used on occasion during this stage, represent the "crossing of a line" in the
personal drug-use of the young person. The youngster is now
planning use of drugs. "Planning" means working out time
and privacy in order to buy drugs, to hide drugs, and to get
high. Buying drugs now replaces using someone else's drugs

when available. The actual use at this stage becomes regular on weekends. As Stage Two develops, drug-use spreads to weeknights and, at the very end of the stage, to occasional weekday use. For the first time, the child uses drugs alone in order to get that good feeling.

Late in this stage, drug-use starts to have small negative consequences. The youngster responds by setting limits on his/her use. "I'll use only on weekends" — "I'll only use pot and alcohol" — "I'll smoke only two joints." Each of these limits or rules is transgressed and soon forgotten by the youngster. The disease progresses.

At some point in this stage, the kid passes a "point of no return" in his dependence on the chemicals. Up to that point, he could quit by his own decision. Beyond that point, he can no longer stop without intensive, external help.

BEHAVIOR.

With Stage Two, progressive changes in behavior occur. The teenager begins to develop pride in "handling" drug-use. There is a desire to identify with the drug-using peer group. The kid is getting into "images." At the same time, the kid is concerned with maintaining good and/or non-interfering relationships with family and school. The result is a dual life. The youngster attempts to maintain a certain appearance and behavior with family and at school. At the same time, he/she is exhibiting another image and set of behaviors with drug-using friends. One street name for this dual life is "Weekend Warrior." The name and lifestyle is lauded in a song by Ted Nugent, a rock musician. This duality also occurs with friendships. Some friends are the old "straight" friends whom parents know. There is another group of friends whom the parents do not know. This "druggie" group will be deliberately kept away from parents. When they call, they will not identify themselves or leave messages. The youngster will often arrange to meet these new friends away from home.

In addition, dramatic and sudden changes in dress occur.

The style will become more "mod," more like "rock band" musicians. Dress will often change from the time the kids leave the house until they join their friends. Typically, a girl will wear a bra when she leaves home, but take it off in a restroom on the way to meet her friends. Hair gets longer, over the eyes, and pants, slacks, shirts, and blouses are tighter, more revealing, and generally sexier. Both boys and girls wear more jewelry.

During this period, parents first notice unexplainable changes in mood. The child will have withdrawn periods alternated with aggressive, angry periods. Solitary times, moodily spent locked in the room with rock music turned up extra loud, are characteristic. Adolescent tantrums and verbal abuse toward parents begin during this stage, and often are dismissed as symptoms of puberty. There will also be a change in language used by the youngster. Not only will current adolescent slang become more frequent, but profanity and verbal abuse will first occur. The kid will also exhibit various forms of charm and deception to cover up his/her dual life. We call this charming behavior "conning." It is, however, plain lying and deception. Late in this stage, the teenager begins stealing to pay for his drugs. This usually begins with theft from parents and siblings.

During this stage, the first signs of something called the "amotivational syndrome" appear. The amotivational syndrome is the progressive loss of motivation, drive, and future orientation on the part of the child. It is characteristic of marijuana use. During the second stage, as the youngster actively seeks the mood swing, he typically will give up hobbies and school extra-curricular activities. These activities require effort and planning which interfere with his recreational drug-use.

Very late in the second stage, school grades drop. Parents usually react to this drop in grades with strong disciplinary action. At this stage, the child will respond to the discipline and bring his grades up one more time. Often the temporary improvement in grades is due to cheating rather than to honest effort. I know of numerous incidents where kids have neatly converted "F's" to "B's" on their report cards. This temporary improvement in academic performance often lulls parents into confidence about the child's situation. It delays necessary action to deal with the child's drug-use.

The behavioral symptoms of the second stage are similar to normal behaviors of adolescence. Parents should avoid the dangers of both over-reaction and non-reaction.

Four guidelines are helpful in assessing teenage behavioral change and drug-use:

1. Change that is sudden, dramatic, and/or radical is an indication of drug-use.
2. Behavior that is drug-use caused is an exaggeration of normal adolescent problems.
3. A combination of behavioral changes together rather than a single change is symptomatic.
4. The drug-using child experiences tension or stress between the two roles he/she is playing in the "dual life."

Late in Stage Two, "blackouts" first occur. One of the effects of mood-altering chemicals is to suppress moral inhibitions that arise from a person's values. The result of drug-use is that a young person will do things in terms of sexuality, theft, vandalism, and deception that violate those normal moral values. When the youngster remembers these violations of values after the effect of the chemical wears off, he/she experiences the first twinges of shame, guilt, and emotional pain. The blackout is a mild form of selective amnesia, which conveniently wipes out memory of behaviors that produce guilt. The youngster does not remember a period in time in which something occurred that was emotionally painful. There is not even memory of the fact that something has been forgotten.

FEELINGS.

During this stage, the teenager experiences euphoric highs. The youngster also experiences mild emotional pain from coming down off the drugs. He begins to experience losses as a result of his chemical use: family, hobbies, school achievement, and dreams. He also begins to experience a discrepancy and conflict between his moral (family) values and his new "druggie" values and behavior. At the beginning of this stage, the youngster by choice seeks the pleasure of feeling good from the drug. As Stage Two develops, the child increasingly chooses to avoid bad feelings by getting high. In time the youngster is no longer able to cope with stress, disappointment, hurt, injustice, or any other emotional difficulties. Therefore, using drugs to feel good, initially a choice, increasingly becomes a necessity.

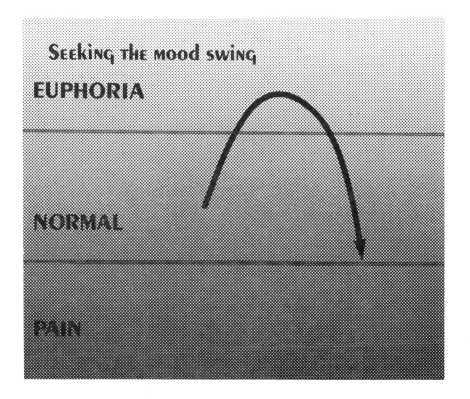

Seeking the mood swing

EUPHORIA

NORMAL

PAIN

By the time an adolescent has moved into Stage Two, he/she has lost the ability to control his/her life and drug-use. Informed and aware parents, school personnel, and counselors are first able to detect drug-use problems during this stage. Parents tend to avoid immediate action. The problem seems mild and hardly distinguishable from our normal expectations of adolescent growth difficulties. The problem is that this delay allows the youngster to progressively worsen and to start suffering serious consequences from drug-use. A child who is sufficiently into Stage Two for the family and other significant adults to detect the problem should be referred for treatment immediately. The child will need outside help: (1) to become drug-free, and (2) to develop those behavioral skills necessary to remain drug-free.

Chapter 9
STAGE THREE –
PREOCCUPATION WITH THE MOOD SWING

Stage Two was characterized by movement from choosing to "do" drugs, to needing to "do" drugs, in order to deal with feelings. Stage Three is the point at which the youngster centers his or her life around getting high. The young person maintains the self-deception of "doing" drugs by personal choice. However, the kid's use of drugs, both to feel good and also to avoid feeling bad, has robbed him/her of those coping mechanisms necessary to handle hurt, fear, anxiety, defeat, injustice, etc. Since the only way the youngster knows to face life is to obtain good feelings by use of chemicals, all other activities fade away in the face of the drug-use obsession.

DRUGS.

For teenagers, alcohol and pot remain the drugs of preference. During Stage Three, the child crosses another line: "moving up" into the use of harder drugs, such as LSD, cocaine, PCP and PHP ("Angel Dust"), THC, MDA, opium, mescaline, etc. Use of "ups" and "downs" and stronger cannabis products is more frequent and in larger quantities. Those kids who see mushrooms as a harder drug begin their use now.

The pattern of use moves from regular weeknights and occasional weekdays to regular weekday use and, finally, at the end of this stage, to being under the almost constant influence of drugs. The kid is "stoned" all the time. Solitary use is more characteristic than social use. The teenager wants to get high, and other people aren't really necessary for this preoccupation.

The costs of getting high are increasing radically. The reason for this is the kid's development of a very high tolerance to the drugs of preference, particularly pot and alcohol. This high tolerance means more drugs are needed to produce the same effect and, therefore, costs increase. During this stage, several "firsts" occur: (1) Usually the first overdose occurs during Stage Three. (2) The kid first realizes he/she has a problem with drug-use. He/she will attempt to "cut down" or stop the use of drugs altogether. These attempts usually fail in a matter of days or weeks. (3) The kid has his/her first experience with "flashbacks." A "flashback" is the experience of being high without having used the drug. At this point, the young person may have "marijuana flashbacks." Later on, "acid flashbacks" become frequent.

Drug-use in the third stage is characterized by preoccupation with getting high, obsession with drug-use, solitary useage, and loss of control over one's use of drugs.

BEHAVIOR.

The drug-use pattern of preoccupation has clear behavioral ramifications. The dual life that was carefully maintained in Stage Two to deceive parents, teachers, and other adults, is now ended. The kid begins to openly identify as a "druggie" with peers. Toward the end of Stage Three, the kid's "druggie" identity is openly exhibited to the adult world, as well as with peers. The teenager begins to dress, use language, have a hairstyle and other lifestyle characteristics which are "druggie" as opposed to "straight." This appearance may include concert T-shirts, marijuana-leaf belt buckles, "coke" spoons on necklaces, longer hair (which is often center-parted), and increased use of slang expressions such as "cool" and "right on, man." In girls, well-worn, skin-tight jeans, seductive halter tops or blouses, and overdone makeup and jewelry may be clues. "Straight" friends are dropped and the youngster's friendships are almost entirely with other openly identified "druggies."

The temporary improvement in school grades under parental pressure in Stage Two now gives way to loss of interest in school. This loss of interest is a continuation of the development of the "amotivational syndrome." The teenager begins to get high before and during the school day. This is accompanied by chronic skipping of school. Being high and skipping classes in turn result in failure at school. Finally, the youngster drops out because going to school interferes with getting high. He/she may be suspended and will simply not return to school. If the teenager is working, he/she gets high at work, starts to miss days at work and, finally, quits or is fired. General lethargy sets in.

Because increased tolerance requires higher expenditures to support one's drug-use, the kids begin to steal — first from parents and later from other people. The stealing reflects itself in shoplifting, theft from "druggie" friends, and possibly breaking-and-entering capers at homes, cars, and businesses. The kid also begins "dealing," which means buying a larger supply of drugs and, in turn, selling them to friends in order to support his or her own increased use. Some girls and a few guys occasionally prostitute themselves to support their useage. During this stage of drug-use, the youngster first becomes involved with the police. The incidents may involve a DWI, possession of drugs, shoplifting, vandalism, breaking and entering, assault and battery, runaway, and other similar types of violations.

Family life becomes a disaster during the third stage. Verbal explosions, abuse, and aggression become chronic. Parents find it impossible to discuss anything, to enforce any rule, or to maintain any kind of communication. The verbal abuse trails into physical violence late in the stage. Kids sneak out of their bedroom windows at night to join "druggie" friends. This soon leads to "splitting" from home and family for the first time.

The first signs of physical deterioration begin in Stage Three. Red eyes, a cough, a sore throat, and appearance of fatigue are common. The youngster develops a chronic marijuana cough, much like the "chain-smoker's cough." Due to suppression of immunity antibodies in his or her body chemistry, the teenager is subject to bronchitis and one cold or virus after another. The youngster seems to slough off frequent illnesses due to his/her lack of physical pain and feeling, since he/she is getting high constantly. Venereal disease is common due to the combination of careless hygiene and sexual promiscuity.

SECOND CHILD PATTERN.

At **Straight,** we have run into consistent difficulty with families concerning an additional adolescent child in the home "doing" drugs. The "second child" has played the "good guy" in contrast to the "druggie" child who is first brought to the. Program. The druggie child serves a "scapegoat" role, focusing the family's attention on his or her behavior. The "second child" underlines this with "conning" comments sympathizing with the parents' problem with the druggie child. Usually the second child keeps attention focused on the scapegoat until very late in Stage Three. Finally, when "preoccupation with drug-use" has dissolved any inhibition about behavior, the family discovers the child's problem. Prior to this late third stage period, we discover the child's drug-use through a sibling interview and a discussion with the first druggie child who is already in the Program. The family responds with strong compulsive denial, holding on to this child's innocence and good behavior. The family's denial is in part rooted in the need of parents to feel some success about their parenting. The second-child pattern is even more difficult to penetrate than the usual Stage Two dual life.

FEELINGS.

The adolescent's life is characterized by desperate preoccupation with getting high. This preoccupation controls the feelings and behavior of the youngster each day. It is, of course, harder to get high due to increased tolerance and higher costs of the drug. Now the youngster feels emotional distress when he is not high. The young person experiences euphoria and actively seeks the euphoric experience of being high. Now, when the youngster comes down, he or she experiences the "backswing into pain." The backswing into pain is emotional rather than physical. However, it is in part due to the physiological experience of "coming down" from the chemical high. The mood-swing into pain is due to the depressant effect of marijuana and its accumulation in the brain. The "coming down" causes depression. It also brings with it the experience of guilt and shame over things done while under the influence of drugs. The guilt and shame is sharper and deeper over sexual behavior, criminal behavior, and relationship behavior. This guilt and shame grows out of the conflict between moral values and behavior.

The pain, particularly from the guilt and shame, causes an eroding of self-worth. Over and over again, I hear kids in the Program say, "I felt like crap," or "I felt like nothing but a piece of crap." Their own self-value is progressively lost to the point of severe negative feelings about self. In order to cope with the hurt, the shame, and the pain, the youngster has to use delusion, rationalization, and deliberate suppression of feelings to get through a day. In turn, the kid requires increased drug-use to wipe out the pain he/she experiences each time he/she comes down. Suicidal thoughts occur for the first time during Stage Three. The kids put together "I am a piece of crap" and "the world sucks" to add up to a painful reality, which results in a willingness to lose life. Overdosing occurs in part as a response to these painful, negative feelings. The adolescent thinks he/she is "different" from his/her "druggie" friends. Everyone else is comfortable. He/she is the only one who is hurting. The experience of living is so distorted that the kid thinks, "I'm going crazy," yet he/she almost never connects the experience of "going

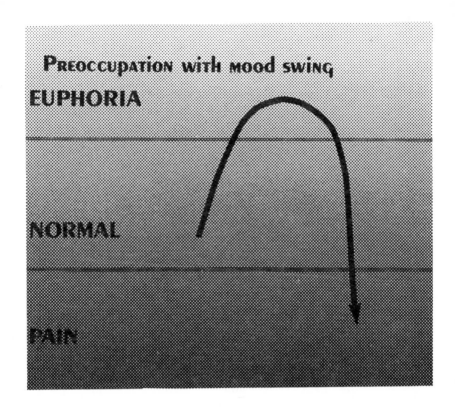

PREOCCUPATION with mood swing

EUPHORIA

NORMAL

PAIN

crazy" with drug-use. Life becomes a constant struggle to be "cool," to keep up his or her "image" of "handling it" and "having fun."

Most families and other helping professionals recognize the child's drug-use some time during Stage Three. The dress, language, lifestyle, and even carelessness about drugs and paraphernalia signals the adult world that the child is in trouble. When adults discover that the child is skipping school chronically, thinking about dropping out of school, or has such negative feelings about himself/herself, it is time to move with deliberate speed to get the child help. Often the adolescent's carelessness about drugs and paraphernalia and about behavior is a deliberate plea for help. He/she is crying out for the adult world to do something to help him/her out of the distress and pain.

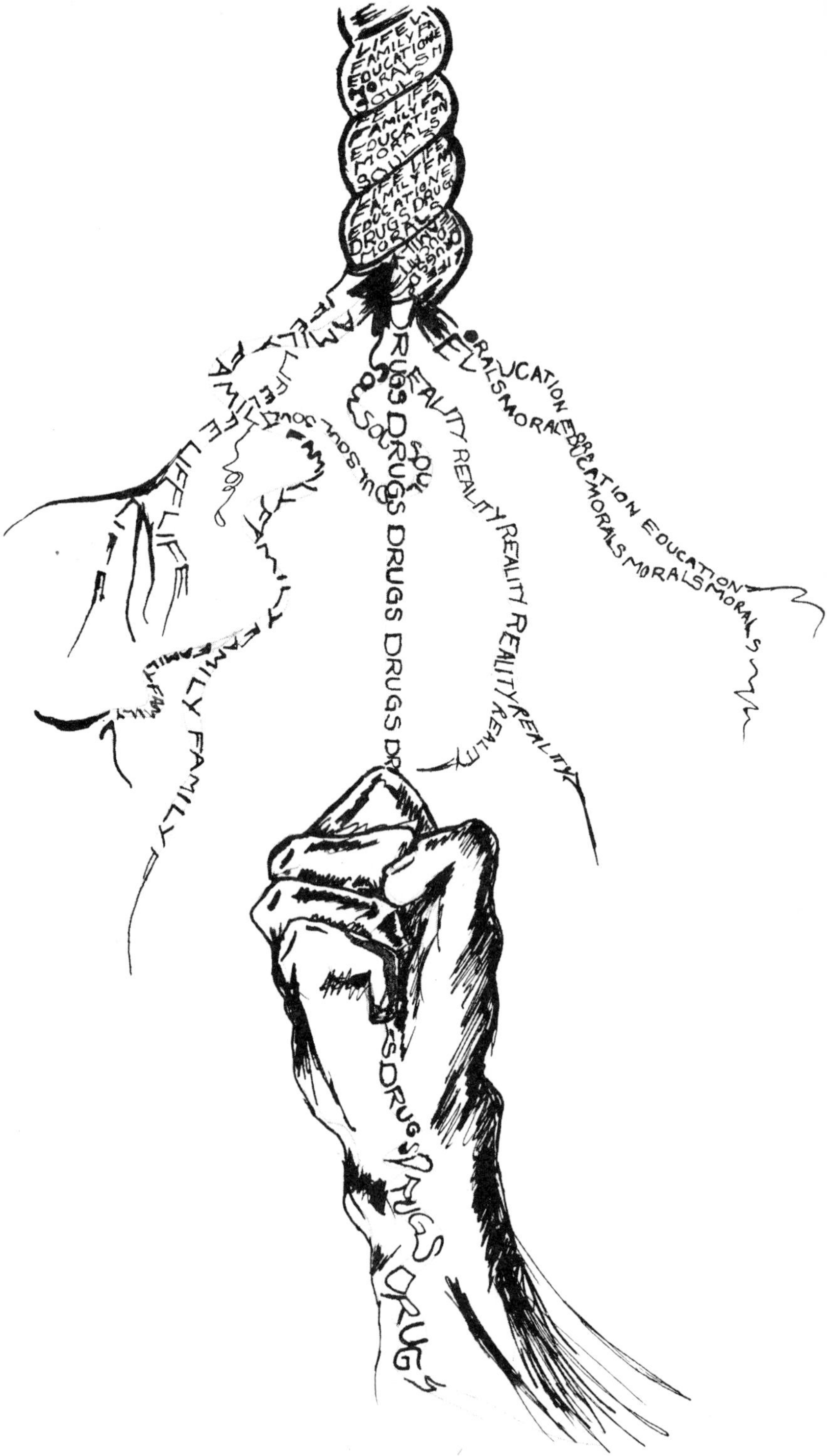

EDUCATION EDUCATION
MORALS MORALS MORALS
REALITY REALITY REALITY REALITY
DRUGS DRUGS DRUGS DRUGS DRUGS DR
FAMILY FAMILY FAMILY
LIFE LIFE LIFE

Chapter 10
STAGE FOUR —
USE OF DRUGS TO FEEL NORMAL ════════════

Stage Four is the final deterioration of life as a result of drug-use. The emotional effects of the drug-use have become so chronic that the youngster feels bad all the time. The young person wakes up in the morning feeling emotional pain. Drugs have to be used in order to produce sufficiently normal feelings for the youngster to function throughout the day. Stage Four is the point at which the teenager has to use drugs in order to function.

DRUGS.

The drugs of preference — alcohol and pot — continue to be used regularly and heavily. In fact, they are used excessively every day. Some teenagers obsessively use one or another of the higher drugs. "Speed Queens," "Acid Freaks," and "Quaalude Queens" all represent specialized compulsive use patterns. Use begins early in the morning as a way of coping with the pain experienced upon awakening. Use is regular throughout the day. The kid can no longer distinguish between feeling "normal" and being "stoned." The young person rarely experiences any good feelings during this stage. Due to emotional deterioration and radically increased tolerance, the euphoric state is rarely, if ever, experienced. The high tolerance results in extremely high costs in order to support one's drug-use. Overdosing occurs with relative frequency due to high tolerance and the compulsive need for drugs. The adolescent has totally lost control over his/her use of drugs.

BEHAVIOR.

The street term for a youngster in Stage Four is a "burn-out." A "burnout" is someone who resembles a zombie. The young person has dull eyes, slow movement, and a generally "wasted" kind of appearance. Since drug-use has become constant and obsessive, the child cannot keep a job, cannot remain in school, or stick to any other regular activity. The deterioration in behavior combined with the high costs and the high tolerance result in frequent trouble with the police and other adult authorities. The youngster's traditional value system is so repressed that he/she continues to engage in social behaviors which cause him/her difficulties. He/she shows no ability to distinguish between acceptable and unacceptable behavior. Behavior includes volcanic anger and aggressive episodes toward family and other people with whom he or she comes into contact. The youngster exhibits severe paranoia: "everyone is out to get him." Blackouts are more frequent and longer in duration. He has "euphoric re-call" of events in his life. In remembering events, he perceives them in a positive, delusional way. He is constantly repressing any show of emotion. When his behavior is not antisocial, it is at least asocial in the sense that his only contact with other people is to obtain drugs and/or the money necessary to purchase drugs.

Physical deterioration is evident. His/her obsession with drugs and their resulting repression of appetite, cause weight loss. Regular pot-smoking causes a loud, chronic marijuana cough, making the youngster sound tubercular. The effects of pot on the immunity system make him/her subject to constant illness. He/she evidences chronic memory loss. He/she may also experience frequent "flashbacks" as a result of "acid" use.

The general description of the fourth stage druggie's life is that he/she looks like a "disaster area." He/she exhibits the walking dead, "burnout" look. A description of the social aspects of his/her life indicate the point to which he/she has deteriorated. The youngster seems to be caught on an emotional roller coaster of drug-use with no way out.

FEELINGS.

Looking at the feeling chart below, the "burnout" wakes up in the morning at the depression/pain point. He/she has to use drugs in order to function and to feel somewhat normal during the day. He/she literally has to take chemicals "to put one foot in front of the other" from morning to night. The drugs produce emotional relief from pain, but no euphoria. Guilt, remorse, shame, and anxiety are chronically present all day. His/her entire living effort is dedicated to obtaining drugs and getting high in order to suppress the chronic pain from these emotions. He/she experiences constant paranoia about people around him/her, and indeed, the whole world. To him/her the world is filled with people who would deny him/her the drugs he/she has come to need with such desperation.

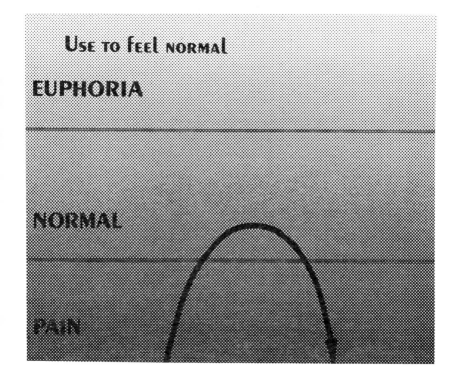

The result of this vicious cycle is almost total destruction of his/her self-worth. The knowledge that the youngster has lost control of his/her life to drugs and the struggle to suppress emotions about things he/she has done, cause his/her self-worth to be eroded almost to nothing. Suicidal ideations come with increasing frequency. After all, life for him/her is a painful, uncontrollable struggle. Why should he/she want to go on living? It becomes difficult for the "burnout" to keep up the facade that he/she is "cool" and that things are good with him/her.

The Stage Four "druggie" is obviously in serious condition emotionally and physically. He/she needs immediate and intensive treatment. The "burnout" youngster takes a much longer period for recovery than do young people who begin treatment while they are in second or third stages of drug-use. First, the fourth-stage youngster takes sixty to ninety days for the drugs to leave the body chemistry and for his/her body chemistry to begin to recover. Second, the effect of prolonged marijuana use seems to affect the range and intensity of feeling states. It is months before such a youngster is able to show much variation in intensity of feeling. This lack of variation in feeling causes some difficulty in treatment. The youngster in this stage also has a series of severe physical health problems as a result of both the drug-use and its encumbering lifestyle. So he/she requires medical evaluation and treatment for these resulting physical illnesses.

The only thing that comes after Stage Four is death. There are a variety of causes for death at the end of this stage, most of which have to do with either emotional or physical deterioration. Drug-use is a terminal disease.

Chapter 11
DRUG-USE IS A FAMILY DISEASE

The previous chapters have described the characteristics and patterns of drug-use as a disease for the individual teenager. The teenager's drug-use has an infective quality in the life of his family. The youngster's feeling state and behavior move from undetectable to disturbing and, finally, to totally disruption of family life.

As the family attempts to cope with the crazy behavior of the child, family members start to do crazy things in response. The kinds of behavior described in the foregoing chapters on the part of the young person are beyond the bounds of normal behavior. The coping mechanisms which families develop, both parents and siblings, to deal with normal family problems, simply do not work with the "druggie" child. Like the "druggie," the family members' lives become increasingly incongruent. Their real feelings are masked by defensive behaviors. This dishonesty causes internal tension and stress in unbelievable proportions. Since the crazy responsive behavior of family members fails to solve the child's problem, the family members, both individually and as a group, develop a strong sense of failure. This failure is felt as anger, rage, hurt, and pain.

The purposes of this book do not require a detailed description of the various sick behaviors family members may choose in order to cope with the "druggie" kid. My purpose in this brief discussion of the family's response to the "druggie" is to point out the effects that the youngster has on the health and well-being of the entire family. The implication is clear: Treatment for the drug-use disease must include the entire family and not just the "druggie" child.

First, the reason for family treatment is the need of each family member for relief from pain. Each parent and each sibling has become diseased in behavior, feelings, and interpersonal communication. They need to become healthy and whole again. Second, the diseased expectations and communications from family members to the recovering "druggie" child make his/her recovery more difficult. If family expectations and responses to the recovering "druggie" child do not change, the child is caught in a bizarre dilemma. He/she must avoid the family, try to treat the family himself/herself, or fall back into his/her family role as a "druggie." If his/her siblings and parents are not treated and he/she is strong enough to continue the recovery, a sibling will take up the "druggie" role.

Individual health and wholeness is important for each family member. Family system health is also important. Each family member's role and relationship must be redefined. Recovery from drug-use is a total family process.

Chapter 12
DRUG-USE IS A TREATABLE DISEASE

When families have a child far enough into drug-use to exhibit problem behavior, parents often panic. As an alternative response, they simply avoid the problem; they deny it. There are several reasons for denial. The first is fear. Most of us have images of "drug addicts" that come from the 50's when only bad, down and out, slum dwellers used drugs such as heroin. Our image is of a "drug addict" who is ninety-five percent incurable. When our child has a problem with drugs, we become afraid that there is no help and, therefore, no hope.

The second reason for panic or avoidance is a sense of failure about our own parenting. We have the need to blame ourselves when our child gets in trouble. The child gets into drugs, so there must be something wrong with our marriage, our family relationship, or our parenting skills. We are afraid to admit it to ourselves, and we are particularly afraid to allow others in our adult peer group to discover what poor parents we really are. The confusion from constant re-evaluation of child-rearing practices since the 60's has contributed to parental insecurity.

Drug-use is a very treatable disease. Over the last decade, a number of people, organizations and programs have proven that both alcoholism and adolescent drug-use can be treated effectively in a vast majority of the cases. Not only the Johnson Institute in Minneapolis, which is a leading training and research organization, but Alcoholics Anonymous, Narcotics Anonymous, and a variety of specific treatment programs have made drug-use a disease from which recovery is possible. There is hope.

The beginning of hope is to be found in bringing reason

to the chaotic situation a "druggie" creates in a family. Up to the point that a family recognizes its child's problem as drugs, the situation seems "insane." Behavior is "insane," feelings are "insane," and communication is impossible. The earlier chapters of this book provide an intelligible framework in which a family can start to understand the child's problem and the family's problem. The behavior which seemed "insane" is still crazy, but now it makes sense because there is a pattern and a cause — the drugs. As parents begin to place the child's use in an intelligible framework, that is, within the framework of the disease concept, they can then begin to take action to solve the problem.

The nature of the treatment process becomes clear when you reflect on the nature of the disease as outlined above. The first step is recognition that drugs are the problem. The second step is placing the youngster in an environment that is "drug-free" for a long enough period of time for that youngster's body chemistry to become "drug-free." The balance of the treatment program involves the young person facing the chronic and permanent nature of the drug-use disease and beginning to take those steps necessary to recover from its effects. Recovery involves making a commitment to remain free of all mood-altering chemicals. It involves facing one's past, all those events that produced guilt, shame, hurt, and pain, and experiencing the feelings for those events that were not felt at the time because of drug-use. Once the past is faced and cleaned out, the child is then able to start learning the skills necessary to remain drug-free and to control effectively his or her own thoughts, feelings, and behavior.

Finally, having learned the skills and begun to practice those skills, the young person develops new behavior and makes that new behavior sufficiently habitual to last for a lifetime. The family goes through a similar process in terms of its secondary and co-dependent role in the disease. The process is simple, direct, and reasonable. There is hope for recovery from drug-use.

"DRUG-USE" REHABILITATION
PROGRAM CRITERIA

The following section is provided to assist families and to help professionals evaluate programs for adolescent drug-users. The criteria listed below provide a beginning point for selection of programs which are effective in assisting young drug-users in their recovery.

1. A Drug-Free Lifestyle

In keeping with the chronic characteristic of this disease, good treatment programs believe that one must become and remain "drug-free" for the rest of his/her life. Many drug programs take compromise positions on social use of marijuana and alcohol. These programs have almost no success in treatment of young people with drug-use problems. In choosing a program for the teenager, make sure that it takes an abstinence position as necessary to recovery.

2. A Drug-Free Environment

One of the main preference drugs of adolescents is marijuana. Delta 9-THC, the main mood-altering ingredient in pot, remains in the brain and nervous tissue for long periods of time after it is used. Delta 9-THC has a fat-soluble nature and our bodies do not have much of a fat-dissolving process. Therefore, it takes a reasonably long period of time for the body chemistry to recover from pot-use and for the youngster to begin to operate at a normal emotional and rational level. A successful program is able to keep the child in a drug-free environment for a minimum of sixty days.

3. Peer Counseling

As Alcoholics Anonymous and other self-help groups have shown us, "those who have the problem" can best be helped by "others who have the problem and are recovering." Given the peer pressure cause of drug-use for most adolescents, a good program uses peer pressure in reverse for recovery. The program should involve "kids helping kids."

4. Family Treatment
Drug-use infects the whole family system. Relationships, communication, behavior, feelings, and self-worth deteriorate. Treating only the drug-user is a design for disaster. Good programs involve the total family, parents and siblings, in treatment from the beginning. Good programs have a recovery program for family members and do not just involve them to help the drug-user recover.

5. An Alcoholics Anonymous Self-Help Mode
Alcoholics Anonymous and similar self-help groups have had a long and successful history of helping people make personal changes in order to recover from addiction and habituation. My belief is that all good programs are based at least in part on the tools of self-change that Alcoholics Anonymous developed. Effective programs also take a strong position that a person has to make the decision to help himself or herself.

6. An Intensive Therapy Process
The best programs seem to have strenuous and intensive therapeutic processes. The drug-use process, with its deterioration of feelings and behavior, is itself a strong disease. Recovery requires a strong and structured approach in order to intervene, arrest, and reverse the effects on one's personal life.

7. Progressive Re-integration
Teenage drug-use is initiated by peer influence and surrounded by a subculture totally enmeshed in drug-use. A good treatment program removes the young person from the cultural-context that says "do drugs" during initial treatment. However, the program should re-integrate the teenager

back into family, school, music, media, dating, leisure time, etc. This "re-integration" should be structured and progressive with appropriate support for his or her new lifestyle.

8. A Cognitive Therapy Mode

Becoming and remaining drug-free involves changing one's thinking, feeling, and behavior. Cognitive and/or rational therapy seems to be most effective in this kind of self-change. This particular therapeutic bias puts heavy responsibility on the individual to do his/her own changing in terms of personal need.

* * *

My hope is that when you, as a helping professional or parent, survey and select a program for a teenage drug-user, the above criteria will help you with questions to ask and with the decision you make.

INTERVENTION.

Drug-use is treatable and recovery is possible. However, someone has to do something to get the kid into treatment. Denial and self-deception are part of the disease for the adolescent. He or she is not going to recognize his/her problem and his/her need for help as long as he/she is in the vicious cycle of emotional pain and drug-induced relief.

Intervention is the active decision by the family to seek help for the young person and itself. "Tough love" means forcing kids into treatment by use of parental authority. After all, they are still children and they are "powerless" over their lives and "insane" behavior while on drugs. Secondly, unlike the alcoholic, the "druggie" is never chemically free of the mood-altering effect of marijuana.

Responsible parents, once they recognize "drug-use" as their child's problem, take action. They find an effective treatment program and then enter their child into that program.

CONCLUSION

Fortunately, drug-use, when detected and diagnosed, is a highly treatable disease. The treatment involves a drug-free atmosphere and intensive therapy for a period of time. Since the child's sense of reality is distorted by the drug-use, it is necessary for parents and professionals to exercise responsible judgment for the child. The adult world has to say "No" to drug-use. A child's drug-use introduces chaos and craziness into the life of the family. The child's crazy behavior and the family's loss of control lead to paralyzing fear.

The beginning of recovery from drug-use is knowledge. The family and other adults involved with young people first must make sense out of the child's behavior. When adults understand that the child's behavior is not random craziness, but the symptoms of drug-use, their sense of fear is eased. The paralysis is broken. Understanding of the child's problem in a coherent framework permits parents to act in the child's behalf. As parents begin to act for their health and the child's health, their initiative itself is a major step in family recovery.

My hope is that this book will help parents and other adults involved with drug-using children find the knowledge necessary to overcome fear and to act in the best interests of the young people.